Best Children's Book on
Composers & Per
(Vol. 1)
by Larry E. Newman

CW01456144

www.musicfunbooks.com

Wolfgang Amadeus Mozart was a very special musician who lived a long time ago.

He was born in Austria in 1756, and from a very young age, he could play the piano and compose his own music.

He was so talented that he even performed for the king and queen of Austria when he was only six years old!

Mozart loved music so much that he wrote over 600 pieces of music in his lifetime. Some of his most famous works are his symphonies, operas, and concertos. He also wrote a lot of music for the piano.

Mozart's music is known for being beautiful and lively. It makes people happy and excited, and sometimes it even makes them want to dance!

When Mozart was only six years old, he played the harpsichord for the queen. She asked him to play a more difficult song, and Mozart said yes! He sat down and played the song perfectly.

The queen was surprised and asked Mozart how he played the song so well. Mozart was quite clever and said, "It's easy. I just use my left hand for the black keys and my right hand for the white keys."

Everyone in the room laughed and clapped for Mozart. From then on, Mozart was known as a child prodigy, which means he was extremely talented at a young age.

Many people still listen to Mozart's music today, and it is often played at concerts and in movies.

Charlie Parker was a famous jazz saxophonist. He was born in Kansas City, Missouri in 1920.

Charlie loved music from a young age, and he learned to play the piano and the alto saxophone when he was just 11 years old.

He is known for inventing a style of jazz called bebop.

Bebop is a type of jazz that is fast-paced and complex. It involves improvising, or making up music on the spot. Charlie Parker was a master at improvising and came up with many new and creative ideas for his music. He was known for his ability to play long and difficult solos.

Charlie Parker worked with other musicians to create bebop, and together they developed a new sound that was different from anything that had been heard before.

Charlie Parker recorded many albums and played with some of the most famous jazz musicians of his time. Some of the musicians he played with include Dizzy Gillespie, Miles Davis, and Thelonious Monk.

One fun fact about Charlie is that he loved to eat chicken. In fact, he was so fond of the bird that he earned the nickname "Yardbird," which was later shortened to "Bird."

Charlie Parker's bebop style of jazz was very popular and influenced many other musicians. It is still played and enjoyed by jazz fans today.

Ludwig van Beethoven was a famous composer who lived a long time ago. He wrote many wonderful pieces of music that are still played and enjoyed today. Beethoven was born in Bonn, Germany in 1770.

He started playing the piano when he was very young, and he was so good at it that he became a famous musician.

One funny thing about Beethoven is that he was really messy. He would often forget where he put his music, and his friends would have to help him find it.

Sometimes he would even write his music on old pieces of paper or napkins because he couldn't find his music notebooks!

Another interesting thing about Beethoven is that he was especially determined. He didn't let anything stop him from making music, even when he became very sick and couldn't hear very well. He would use special tools to help him write his music, and he kept writing incredible pieces until the end of his life.

Today, Beethoven is remembered as one of the greatest composers of all time. His music is played all over the world, and people of all ages enjoy listening to it. So the next time you hear one of Beethoven's famous symphonies, remember the fun and interesting things about this amazing composer!

Elvis Presley was a very famous singer and actor. He was known for his amazing voice and his cool dancing moves.

He was born in Tupelo, Mississippi on January 8, 1935.

Elvis grew up listening to different types of music, and he loved singing and playing the guitar. He started his music career when he was just a teenager, and he quickly became popular.

One of the things that made Elvis so special was his unique style. He had long, wavy hair and he liked to wear flashy, colorful clothes.

He also had a guitar that he called "Baby," and he would play it on stage while he sang. Elvis liked to dance on stage, too - including swinging his hips and shaking his legs. He got into trouble for this since some people thought it set a bad example for young people.

Elvis was also known for his love of peanut butter and banana sandwiches. He would eat them all the time, and they became one of his favorite snacks.

Despite his success, Elvis was an especially humble person. He always gave back to the community and helped those in need. He also loved spending time with his family and friends.

In the end, Elvis will always be remembered as one of the greatest musicians of all time.

Johann Sebastian Bach was a famous musician who lived a long time ago. He was born in Germany in 1685 and he lived until 1750. Bach was a very talented man and he wrote a lot of fantastic music.

One of the things that made Bach so special was that he could play many different instruments. He was a master of the organ, which is a big instrument with lots of pipes and buttons that you can use to make lots of different sounds. Bach also played the violin, which is a small instrument that you hold under your chin and play with a bow.

Bach's music was quite complex and sometimes it was hard to understand. Even though it was hard, it was still very beautiful. Bach wrote a lot of music for the church, and he also wrote some music for the king.

One of the funniest things about Bach is that he had 20 children! Can you imagine having 20 kids? That's a lot of kids to take care of! Bach must have been really busy taking care of his kids and writing music at the same time.

Despite having so many kids, Bach still managed to write some of the most gorgeous and complex music that has ever been written. He was a true genius, and his music is still enjoyed by people all over the world today.

Louis Armstrong was a famous musician who played the trumpet and sang.

He was born in New Orleans, Louisiana on August 4th, 1901 and loved music from a very young age.

He began playing the trumpet when he was just 11 years old. He quickly became a master of the trumpet and was known for his unique and lively style of playing.

One funny thing about Louis was that he had a low, deep and gravelly voice, which made him sound like a grown-up even when he was a little boy.

This made his friends and family laugh, but it also made him stand out as a musician.

Louis became very famous and traveled all over the world to play his music. He even performed for the president of the United States!

But despite all of his fame and success, Louis never forgot where he came from. He always stayed true to his roots and continued to play the music of New Orleans, even as he became a world-famous star.

Louis Armstrong was a truly special musician who brought joy and happiness to people all over the world. His music will live on forever, and we will never forget the unique and wonderful sound of his trumpet.

Frédéric Chopin was a famous musician who lived a long time ago.

He was from Poland, and he played the piano really well. In fact, some people say he was the best piano player ever!

Chopin was born in 1810, and he started playing the piano when he was just a little boy. He was so good at it that he gave his first public concert when he was only eight years old. Can you imagine playing the piano in front of lots of people when you were that young?

Chopin wrote lots of lovely music for the piano. Some of his pieces are called "nocturnes" because they sound soft and dreamy, like they would be played at night. Other pieces are called "etudes" because they are really hard to play and they help piano players practice their skills.

Even though Chopin lived a long time ago, people still love to listen to his music. In fact, if you go to a piano recital, you might hear someone play a piece by Chopin. And if you close your eyes, you might feel like you're traveling back in time to when Chopin was alive and playing his beautiful music.

Richard Rogers was a famous American composer who wrote many popular songs and musicals.

One of his most famous songs was "Oh, What a Beautiful Morning" from the musical Oklahoma!

Rogers was born in New York City in 1902 and grew up loving music. He learned to play the piano and eventually went to college to study music.

After college, he started working in the theater and writing music for plays and musicals.

One of the things that made Rogers so special was that he could write both the music and the lyrics for his songs. This made his songs even more fun and exciting to listen to.

One funny story about Rogers is that he was once asked to write a song for a cow in a play. The cow was supposed to sing a happy song about how much she loved being a cow. Rogers wrote the song and it turned out to be a big hit. The cow even got to sing it on Broadway!

Rogers was a very talented composer and his songs continue to be enjoyed by people of all ages. His music has brought joy and happiness to millions of people around the world.

Pyotr Ilyich Tchaikovsky was a famous composer who was born in Russia and grew up to be very talented. One of the most famous things he wrote was a ballet called The Nutcracker, which is about a girl named Clara who goes on an adventure with a nutcracker that comes to life.

Tchaikovsky was a hard worker and spent a lot of time practicing and perfecting his music. He was also quite shy and didn't like to perform in front of people very much. But even though he was shy, his music was so amazing that it made people happy and excited to hear it.

One funny thing about Tchaikovsky is that he loved candy! He would eat so much candy that his friends would tease him and call him "Tchaikovsky the Candy Man." But Tchaikovsky didn't mind because he loved candy so much.

Pyotr Ilyich Tchaikovsky was a talented composer who wrote very special music that is still enjoyed by people today. Even though he was shy, his music was so good that it made people happy.

And if you ever see a performance of The Nutcracker, make sure to listen carefully because you might just hear some of Tchaikovsky's music!

Ella Fitzgerald was a famous singer who was known for her beautiful voice and ability to sing a wide range of music. She was born in 1917 in Virginia, and grew up in New York City.

When Ella was a young girl, she loved to sing.

She would often sing along to the songs she heard on the radio, and even enter singing contests. One time, she entered a contest at the famous Apollo Theater in Harlem, and ended up winning! This was a big moment for Ella, and it helped launch her career as a professional singer.

Ella went on to become one of the most famous and beloved singers of all time. She sang with some of the biggest names in jazz and pop music, and even won 13 Grammy Awards. She was also known for her amazing sense of humor, and would often tell jokes and make her audiences laugh.

One of Ella's most famous jokes was about her own singing ability. She would say, "I may not be the best singer in the world, but I'm the best Ella Fitzgerald there is!" This shows how confident and humble she was, and how much she loved to make people smile.

Ella Fitzgerald was a talented and funny singer who will always be remembered for her incredible voice and charming personality. She was a true star, and her music continues to inspire people of all ages.

The Beatles were a really famous band from a long time ago. They were from a place called England, and they made lots of songs that lots of people still know and like today.

One thing that was really cool about the Beatles was their hair. They had long, shaggy hair, and it was very different from what most people were used to seeing back then. This made them stand out, and it helped make them even more famous.

Another thing that was cool about the Beatles was the way they played their instruments. They had a guitar, a bass guitar, a drum, and a keyboard. They played these instruments together, and they made beautiful music.

One of the most famous Beatles songs is called "Twist and Shout." It's a fun song, and it's still played at parties and dances today. If you ever hear it, you should try to dance along!

The Beatles were a really important and cool band. They would play their songs on the radio and people would listen and feel happy.

Sometimes when people are feeling sad, they will listen to music to make them feel better. The Beatles were really good at doing that.

They made lots of great music, and they had unique hair and cool instruments. They're still remembered and loved today by millions of people around the world.

George Frideric Handel was a famous composer who lived a long time ago.

He was born in Germany and moved to England when he was a young man.

Handel was a very talented musician and he wrote many memorable pieces of music. Some of his most famous works include the "Messiah" and "Water Music".

One interesting thing about Handel and the other men of his time was that they all wore wigs. In those days, wigs were very popular and many people wore them to show off their wealth and status.

Handel was no exception - he had a big, fluffy wig that he wore everywhere he went.

But despite his fancy wig, Handel was an especially humble and kind man. He was known for his generosity and he often gave his money to charity. He was also a big animal lover and he had a pet cat named Puff.

George Frideric Handel was a talented composer who wrote many beautiful pieces of music. He was also a kind and generous man who loved animals. And, like many other men of his time, he wore a wig to show off his wealth and status.

John Williams is a famous American composer who has written music for many movies and TV shows. One of his most famous pieces is the Star Wars theme. It's the music that plays when the Star Wars movies start, and it's very exciting and dramatic.

When John Williams was young, he loved to play the piano. He went to college to study music and became a great composer.

He has won many awards for his music, including five Oscars.

One fun fact about John Williams is that he has written music for all the Star Wars movies except for one. Can you guess which one? It's Star Wars: The Clone Wars!

John Williams' music is very special because it can make us feel happy, sad, or scared, just by listening to it. It's like magic! And his Star Wars music is especially epic. It makes us feel like we are flying through space on a spaceship, battling evil and saving the galaxy.

If you haven't heard John Williams' music before, you should definitely listen to it. It will take you on an adventure, right from your own living room!

Joseph Haydn was a famous composer who lived a long time ago. He wrote a lot of music for different instruments, including the piano and the violin. One of the things that made his music special was that he liked to include jokes and surprises in it.

For example, in his string quartet in E flat major, Haydn would sometimes make the audience think the music was over when it wasn't. He would do this by writing a section that sounded like the end of the piece, but then he would add more music after it. This trick is called a "false ending" and it would make the audience laugh because they were surprised.

Haydn was known as the "Father of the String Quartet" and sometimes people called him Papa Haydn.

Haydn was also a teacher and one of his students was a famous composer named Ludwig van Beethoven. Beethoven learned a lot from Haydn and went on to become a great composer himself.

Haydn was a very clever composer and he liked to make people happy with his music. He wrote many different kinds of pieces, from fast and energetic ones to slow and gentle ones. He also wrote a lot of music for the choir and the orchestra.

His music is still played and enjoyed by people all around the world.

Leonard Bernstein was a very famous American composer who wrote lots of music for the TV and the concert hall.

He is known for many different kinds of music, but one of his most famous compositions is called West Side Story.

West Side Story is a musical about two young lovers, Tony and Maria, who come from different neighborhoods in New York City. Tony is from the "West Side," while Maria is from the "East Side." The two neighborhoods don't get along, and the story is about how Tony and Maria try to overcome their differences and be together.

Bernstein was also known for creating a TV show called The Young People's Concerts. This show was special because it was all about classical music, but it was made for kids to watch and enjoy. Bernstein conducted many episodes of the show, and he made the music fun and interesting for kids.

As a conductor, Bernstein was known for his energetic and passionate conducting style. He worked with many famous orchestras, including the New York Philharmonic and the Boston Symphony Orchestra.

Leonard Bernstein was a very important figure in the world of music, and his work is still enjoyed by people today. He will always be remembered as a great conductor and composer.

Clara Schumann was a very special musician. She was a German composer and teacher, and she was also a pianist. Clara was born in 1819, and she started playing the piano when she was only nine years old.

She was so good at it that she gave her first piano concert when she was only eleven.

Clara Schumann was a hard worker. She practiced the piano for many hours every day, and she also wrote music.

She wrote over 100 pieces of music, including piano solos and songs. Clara also taught many students how to play the piano.

One funny thing about Clara is that she loved chocolate. She would often eat a piece of chocolate before she played the piano, to help her relax. Sometimes, she would even hide chocolate under the piano so she could sneak a bite while she was playing.

Clara Schumann was a very important musician. She was one of the first women to be a successful composer and pianist. She inspired many other musicians, and her music is still enjoyed by people all around the world today.

Duke Ellington was a very famous musician. He was born in Washington D.C. in 1899, and he started playing the piano when he was only seven years old and he quickly became one of the best musicians in the world.

Duke Ellington was known for his jazz music. He played the piano and also wrote music. He wrote over 1,000 pieces of music, including songs, piano solos, and music for orchestras.

Duke also led his own band, and they played at many concerts and festivals.

One funny thing about Duke Ellington is that he loved to tell jokes. He would often tell jokes to his band members and his audience during concerts.

Duke was also very smart and he loved to learn new things. He even learned how to speak French and Italian.

Duke Ellington was a really important musician. He was one of the first musicians to make jazz music popular around the world.

Today, many people still enjoy listening to his music, and he is considered one of the greatest musicians of all time.

Antonio Vivaldi was a famous musician who was born in Italy in 1678. Vivaldi was a very talented man and he could play many different instruments, but he was best known for playing the violin.

One of the things that made Vivaldi's music special was that he wrote a lot of music for the seasons. He wrote four pieces of music, one for each season, and each one was named after the season it represented. For example, his Spring piece had a lot of happy, lively music in it, and his Winter piece had slow, sad music.

Vivaldi was an especially famous musician during his time, and he even wrote music for the king of France. But not everyone liked his music. Some people thought it was too loud and noisy.

But Vivaldi didn't let that stop him. He kept on writing and playing his beautiful music for anyone who would listen.

Today, Vivaldi's music is still enjoyed by people all over the world. It is fun to listen to, and it can make you feel happy, sad, or even a little bit scared. But no matter what, Vivaldi's music is always exciting and full of life.

Yo Yo Ma is a very famous musician who plays the cello.

The cello is a big, wonderful sounding instrument that looks a bit like a violin, but it is much bigger and has a deeper sound.

Yo Yo Ma is now one of the best cellists in the world.

Yo Yo Ma was born in Paris, France, but he grew up in the United States. He started playing the cello when he was only four years old, and he was so good at it that he gave his first public concert when he was only seven.

From then on, he kept practicing and getting better and better, and now he is one of the most famous musicians in the world.

Yo Yo Ma's parents were both musicians and began lessons with Ma at age 3. By age 5, he had memorized three of Johann Sebastian Bach's solo suites. At age 7, he played for President Kennedy and by age 16 he was in college at Harvard University.

Yo Yo Ma has recorded more than 100 albums, and he has won many awards for his music. He has also played with many other famous musicians, including the great composer John Williams.

Yo Yo Ma's music is loved by people of all ages, and he is known for his exceptionally expressive playing.

Antonin Dvorak was a famous composer from a long time ago. He was born in a small town in Czechoslovakia.

Dvorak loved music from a very young age and started playing the violin when he was just a little boy.

He was so talented that he started composing his own music when he was only a teenager.

One of Dvorak's most famous pieces of music is called the "New World Symphony." It's named that because Dvorak wrote it when he came to America. He spent some time in a place called New York City, where he wrote the music.

The "New World Symphony" is a really beautiful piece of music that lots of people still enjoy listening to today.

But Dvorak wasn't just a serious composer. He also had a great sense of humor. He once wrote a piece of music called the "Humoresque," which is a funny word that means "jokes."

The "Humoresque" is a lively and playful piece of music that makes you want to dance and have fun.

Dvorak was an incredibly important composer and his music is still enjoyed by people all over the world. He showed us that even if you come from a small town, you can do big things if you work hard and follow your dreams.

Claude Debussy was a famous composer from France. He lived a long time ago, but people still listen to his music today because it's so beautiful.

Debussy was a very talented musician and started playing the piano when he was just a little boy.

He was so good at it that he went to a special music school to learn even more.

One of Debussy's most famous pieces of music is called "Clair de Lune," which means "moonlight" in French. It's a very calming and peaceful piece of music that makes you feel like you're floating on a cloud. Debussy wrote it when he was sitting by a lake at night, looking up at the moon. It's like he took the beauty of the night sky and turned it into music.

But Debussy wasn't just a serious composer. He also had a great sense of humor. He once wrote a piece of music called "Golliwog's Cakewalk," which is a funny name for a silly dance. The "Golliwog's Cakewalk" is a very playful and energetic piece of music that makes you want to get up and move.

Debussy was an important composer and his music is still enjoyed by people all over the world. He showed us that music can be beautiful and fun at the same time. And he also taught us that you don't have to be grown up to make wonderful music – you just have to have a passion for it.

Hans Zimmer is a very famous composer who writes music for movies. He was born in Germany, but now he lives in Los Angeles, where a lot of movies are made. He's written music for some of the biggest and most popular movies in the world.

One of Zimmer's most famous pieces of music is from a movie called "The Lion King." It's a very emotional piece of music that makes you feel like you're in the middle of the African savannah, watching the animals roam.

Zimmer wrote the music for "The Lion King" when he was on vacation in Africa, and he was inspired by the sounds of the animals and the beauty of the landscape.

But Zimmer isn't just a serious composer. He also has a great sense of humor. He once wrote a piece of music for a movie called "The Pirates of the Caribbean," which is a funny and adventurous story about pirates. The music for "The Pirates of the Caribbean" is very playful and lively, and it makes you want to sail the seas and hunt for treasure.

Zimmer is a really important composer and his music is enjoyed by people all over the world. He shows us that music can make a movie even more exciting and emotional. And he teaches us that you don't have to be a pirate to enjoy a good adventure – you just have to have a sense of fun.

Aaron Copland was a famous American composer. He was born on November 14, 1900, in Brooklyn, New York. He wrote many different kinds of music, but he is best known for his Americana style, which is music that sounds like America.

One of his most famous pieces is called "Appalachian Spring." It's named after a place in the United States called the Appalachian Mountains.

The music is quite grand and sounds like the mountains. It's like a big, happy, outdoor adventure!

Another one of his pieces is called "Rodeo." It's named after a sport that people do on horseback in the West. The music is very exciting and makes you want to ride a horse!

Aaron Copland was a very talented composer. He wrote music for orchestras, piano, and even movies. He also taught other people how to write music.

He was an especially nice person, too. Once, a little girl asked him to autograph her music book. He was happy to do it, and even wrote a special message just for her. He said, "To my little friend, keep on making beautiful music!"

Aaron Copland lived to be 90 years old. He died on December 2, 1990. But his music lives on and is still enjoyed by people all over the world.

Camille Saint-Saëns was a famous French composer. He was born in Paris in 1835 and started playing the piano when he was just three years old.

By the time he was five, he was already composing his own music.

Saint-Saëns wrote many different kinds of music, but he is most famous for his symphonies and concertos.

He also wrote a lot of music for the piano, and some of his pieces are still played by pianists today.

One of Saint-Saëns' most famous pieces is called "The Carnival of the Animals." It's a fun and silly piece of music that was inspired by a trip he took to the zoo. In the music, each animal has its own tune, and you can imagine them all marching around in a big parade.

Saint-Saëns was a very talented musician, and he worked hard to perfect his craft. He even invented a new type of organ that had a lot more keys than the ones that were used at the time.

Saint-Saëns was a true master of music, and he left behind a wonderful legacy of beautiful pieces for us to enjoy. So next time you listen to some of his music, think of the little boy who loved to play the piano and grew up to be a great composer.

George Gershwin was an American composer who wrote some of the most famous music in the world.

He was born in Brooklyn, New York in 1898, and he started playing the piano when he was just a little boy.

Gershwin wrote a lot of different kinds of music, but he is best known for his songs and his symphonic jazz pieces.

One of his most famous songs is called "Rhapsody in Blue," and it's a fun and lively piece that always gets people dancing.

In addition to writing music, Gershwin also wrote plays and musicals. One of his most famous musicals is called "Porgy and Bess," and it tells the story of two poor people living in the city. It's a touching story that has been enjoyed by millions of people all over the world.

Gershwin was a very talented composer, and he loved making music that made people happy. He once said, "I try to make my music say what words cannot." And that's exactly what he did with his wonderful songs and symphonies.

So next time you hear some of Gershwin's music, remember the little boy from Brooklyn who grew up to be one of the greatest composers of all time. And don't be afraid to get up and dance along!

Johannes Brahms was a famous German composer who wrote some of the most beautiful music in the world. He was born in Hamburg, Germany in 1833, and he started playing the piano when he was just a little boy.

Brahms wrote a lot of different kinds of music, but he is best known for his symphonies and his concertos. One of his most famous symphonies is called Symphony No. 1, and it's a big, grand piece of music that sounds like a big adventure.

In addition to writing music, Brahms also loved to play the piano. He was a very talented pianist, and he would often play his own music for his friends. One time, he even played a trick on his friends by pretending to be two different pianists at the same time. He would sit at the piano and play with his left hand, while his right hand was hidden behind his back. His friends were amazed when they realized what he was doing!

Brahms was a truly gifted composer, and he left behind a wonderful legacy of incredible music for us to enjoy. So next time you listen to some of his symphonies or piano concertos, think of the little boy who loved to play the piano and grew up to be a great composer.

Igor Stravinsky was a famous Russian composer who wrote some of the most exciting and energetic music in the world.

He was born in St. Petersburg, Russia in 1882, and he started playing the piano when he was just a little boy.

Stravinsky wrote a lot of different kinds of music, but he is best known for his ballets and his symphonies. One of his most famous ballets is called "The Firebird," and it's a thrilling and magical story about a brave prince who saves a beautiful princess from a wicked sorcerer.

In addition to writing music, Stravinsky also loved to play practical jokes on his friends. One time, he even put a fake snake in a friend's bed to surprise him. His friend was so scared that he jumped out of bed and ran out of the room!

Stravinsky was a very talented composer, and he was always looking for new and exciting ways to write music. He once said, "The musician is perhaps the most modest of animals, but he is also the proudest. It is he who invented the sublime art of ruining poetry."

So next time you listen to some of Stravinsky's music, think of the little boy who loved to play the piano and grew up to be a great composer. And don't forget to watch out for any sneaky snakes!

Count Basie was a famous jazz musician who played the piano and led a big band. He was born in New Jersey in 1904 and started playing music when he was a kid. When he grew up, he formed his own band and played all around the world.

Count Basie's band traveled mostly by bus, and they had a lot of fun together on the road. They would often stop at interesting places and have adventures along the way. One time, they stopped at a petting zoo and got to pet and feed the animals. Another time, they visited a theme park and rode all the fun rides.

Count Basie was known for his swingin' style and his ability to get people to dance. He was also a very good leader and made sure everyone in his band was happy. Count Basie's band played at lots of fancy places, like the White House and Carnegie Hall, but they also played at smaller clubs and schools. No matter where they played, people always had a great time listening to their music.

Count Basie was a very talented musician and made a lot of people happy with his music. He was inducted into the Rock and Roll Hall of Fame in 1987, and his music is still enjoyed by people today.

If you ever get the chance to listen to some of Count Basie's music, make sure to give it a listen - you won't be disappointed!

Nadia Boulanger and Lili Boulanger were two very talented musicians from France. Nadia was a composer, conductor, and teacher, while Lili was a composer. Nadia was the older sister and Lili was the younger one.

Even though they were sisters, they had very different talents. Nadia was known for her skills as a teacher and for helping young musicians develop their talents. She taught many famous composers and musicians, including Aaron Copland, Quincy Jones, and Philip Glass. Nadia was also a composer and wrote music in a variety of styles, including classical, opera, and ballet.

Lili, on the other hand, was known for her talent as a composer. She was able to write beautiful and expressive music that touched people's hearts. Lili was a member of the French Academy of Fine Arts and won several awards for her compositions.

Even though Lili was not as well-known as Nadia during her lifetime, her music has gained more recognition in recent years and she is now considered an important figure in the history of classical music.

While Nadia and Lili had different talents, they were both really talented musicians. They worked hard and created beautiful music that will be enjoyed by people for many years to come. They were truly special musicians who left a lasting legacy through their music.

Quincy Jones is a famous musician and music producer. He has worked with many famous artists, including Michael Jackson and Frank Sinatra. He was born in 1933 in Chicago.

When he was a teenager, he played the trumpet and went to college to study music. After college, he started working in the music industry and has had a long and successful career.

Quincy Jones has won many awards for his music, including 27 Grammy Awards. He is known for his talent as a conductor, composer, and arranger. He has also produced many hit songs and albums.

In addition to his work in music, Quincy Jones has also been involved in television and film. He has produced and directed several movies and TV shows.

But Quincy isn't just about making music. He is also a big supporter of education and helping others. He has started a foundation to help young people learn about music and the arts.

He has worked to raise money for charities and has supported many causes, including education and the arts.

Quincy Jones is a talented and successful musician and producer. He has made a big impact on the music industry and has helped many people through his philanthropy work.

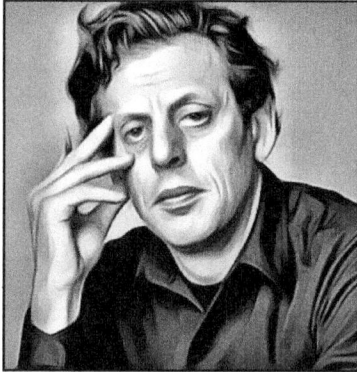

Phillip Glass is a famous composer who has written lots of music that people all around the world enjoy. He was born in Baltimore, Maryland in 1937 and started playing the piano when he was just six years old.

Phillip Glass has composed all sorts of music, like classical, opera, and even music for movies. One of his most famous works is an opera called "Einstein on the Beach." It was performed for the first time in 1976 and has been performed lots of times since then.

Phillip Glass is known for his special style of music called minimalism. This means his music often has simple, repeating patterns and a limited number of notes. It creates a feeling of calm and focus, and lots of people find it very relaxing to listen to.

In addition to composing music, Phillip Glass has also written books and given talks about music at universities. He has won lots of awards for his work, like a Pulitzer Prize in Music and a lifetime achievement award from the National Endowment for the Arts.

Phillip Glass is still composing music today and his work is still enjoyed by people of all ages. If you haven't listened to any of his music yet, you should give it a try. You might just discover that it's one of your favorite things to listen to!

Scott Joplin was a famous musician who lived a long time ago. He was born in 1868 and grew up in Texas. Scott Joplin was known for playing the piano and composing music. He was very good at it and his music was loved by many people.

One of Scott Joplin's most famous pieces of music is called "The Maple Leaf Rag." It was published in 1899 and became very popular. People loved to dance to it and it was played at parties and events all over the country. "The Maple Leaf Rag" is still played today and is considered a classic piece of American music.

Scott Joplin's music was called "ragtime," which was a new type of music that was popular in the late 1800s and early 1900s. It was a mix of African American and European music and had a fast, upbeat tempo. Scott Joplin's music was so popular that he became known as the "King of Ragtime."

Scott Joplin's music was not only popular in America, but it was also enjoyed by people all around the world. He traveled to Europe and played his music for audiences there. Scott Joplin's music is still enjoyed by people today and is a important part of America's musical history.

If you're a fan of music and like to dance, you should definitely give Scott Joplin's music a listen. You'll love the catchy rhythms and fun beats. Who knows, you might even find yourself tapping your feet and dancing along to the music of the "King of Ragtime"!

Maurice Ravel was a famous composer who lived a long time ago. He was born in France and grew up learning how to play the piano and other instruments.

Ravel was known for his beautiful and intricate music, which was inspired by many different cultures and styles.

One of Ravel's most famous pieces is called "Bolero." This music starts out slow and quiet, and then it gets louder and faster as it goes on.

"Bolero" is like a big party on a dance floor! Ravel also wrote music for the ballet, which is a type of dance performance with pretty costumes and lots of movement. One of his ballet pieces is called "Daphnis and Chloe."

Ravel was a very talented musician, and he traveled all around the world to perform his music. He even went to America to play for President Woodrow Wilson! Ravel was also a good friend of another famous composer named Claude Debussy. Together, they helped create a new style of music called "Impressionism." This style uses lots of different sounds and colors to create a mood or feeling.

Ravel's music is still played and enjoyed by people all over the world today. If you ever get the chance to hear some of his music, you'll really like it. It's beautiful, exciting, and full of surprises.

Toshiko Akioshi is a jazz musician from Japan. She is a pianist and composer and leads her own jazz big band. Toshiko was born in 1929 in Dairen, China.

When she was a little girl, her family moved to Japan.

She started playing the piano when she was only five years old. When she grew up, she went to college to study music.

She became the first Japanese student to attend the Berklee School of Music in Boston where she received a full scholarship.

One special aspect of her music is that it has a lot of different layers and textures, which means that there are many different sounds happening at the same time and they all blend together to create a rich and complex sound.

Another special feature of Toshiko's music is that it is often influenced by Japanese culture. She incorporates traditional Japanese music and instruments into her compositions, and sometimes even writes music that tells stories about Japanese history or culture.

Toshiko's music is very interesting and different from other types of music, and people who enjoy listening to it appreciate the way that she blends together different sounds and cultural influences.

Arnold Schoenberg was a famous composer who was born in 1874 in Austria. He wrote operas, symphonies, concertos and more.

One of the things that made Arnold special was that he liked to try new things in his music.

He didn't just stick to the same old sounds and melodies that other composers used. Instead, he experimented with new ways of arranging notes and rhythms.

He even invented a new system for writing music called the "twelve-tone system."

The "twelve-tone system" is a way of writing music that uses all 12 notes of the musical scale in a special order. Each note is played one time before any of the notes are played again. This helps to make the music sound very organized and balanced.

Despite being a little bit different from other composers, Arnold Schoenberg's music was very popular and is still played and enjoyed today.

Thanks to composers like Arnold Schoenberg, the world of music is full of wonderful surprises and exciting new sounds. Even if you're not familiar with a particular composer or piece of music, it's always worth giving it a listen. You never know what you might discover!

Dizzy Gillespie was a famous jazz musician who was born in South Carolina in 1917. He played the trumpet and was known for his unique style and sound. Gillespie was one of the pioneers of a type of jazz called bebop, which was known for its fast tempo and complex melodies.

Gillespie began playing music when he was a young boy, and he quickly became skilled at the trumpet. As he got older, he played with many different bands and orchestras, and he even started his own group called the Dizzy Gillespie Orchestra.

Gillespie was not only a talented musician, but he was also a showman. He was known for his wild and energetic performances, and he often wore flashy clothes and big hats on stage. Gillespie loved to make people laugh and have a good time, and his music was always full of energy and excitement.

One of the things that made Gillespie's music so special was his use of unusual instruments and techniques. For example, he liked to play the trumpet using a technique called "bent notes," where he would bend the pitch of the notes by moving his lips and tongue in a certain way. He also played the trumpet with a curved bell, which gave his sound a unique and distinct quality.

Gillespie was a true legend in the world of jazz, and his music continues to be enjoyed by people of all ages today.

Béla Bartók was a famous composer and musician from Hungary. He was born in 1881. Bartók was a very talented pianist and composer. He wrote many pieces of music that are still played and enjoyed today.

One thing that made Bartók special was that he was interested in the folk music of his home country, Hungary. He spent a lot of time traveling so that he could collect folk songs and dances. He used these folk melodies in his own compositions, which helped to make his music unique and different from other classical music.

Bartók also composed music for the piano, and many of his piano pieces are very challenging to play. They require a lot of skill and practice to perform well. Some of Bartók's most famous piano works include "Mikrokosmos," "For Children," and "Sonata for Two Pianos and Percussion."

In addition to his work as a composer and pianist, Bartók was also a teacher. He taught music at the Budapest Academy of Music and helped to train many talented musicians.

Bartók's music has been enjoyed by people all over the world, and he is still considered one of the greatest composers of the 20th century. His compositions have a special place in the hearts of many classical music lovers, and his unique style and use of folk music continue to inspire and influence musicians today.

Frank Sinatra was a famous singer and actor who was born in Hoboken, New Jersey in 1915.

Frank's big start in music came when he joined the Tommy Dorsey Band in the 1940s. Frank became the lead singer of the band.

Frank's time with the Tommy Dorsey Band helped him become a well-known singer and launched his solo career. Frank went on to release many albums and have many hit songs as a solo artist. He also acted in movies and television shows, and won an Academy Award for his role in the film "From Here to Eternity."

Frank was also known for his sense of style and his love of performing. He was often seen wearing a tuxedo and sang with a lot of energy and passion. He performed for millions of people around the world and was loved by his fans for his talent and charisma.

Frank was a very important figure in the history of popular music. He helped popularize a style of singing called crooning, which is when a singer sings in a soft, smooth voice.

He also helped bring swing music, a type of jazz, to a wider audience. Frank's music and style influenced many other singers and musicians, and he is still remembered as one of the greatest singers of all time.

Jean Sibelius was a famous composer who lived a long time ago. He was born in Finland. Sibelius was a very talented musician and started playing the violin when he was a child. As he grew older, Sibelius became more and more interested in composing music.

He wrote many beautiful pieces for the violin, as well as for orchestras and choirs including "Finlandia" and "Valse Triste."

Sibelius was also very interested in nature and often took long walks in the forest near his home. He loved the trees and the animals and often used them as inspiration for his music. Sibelius's love for nature can be heard in the peaceful and calming melodies of his compositions.

Sibelius was also a big supporter of Finland's independence and wrote music to celebrate the country's freedom.

Sibelius was a kind and gentle man. He had a wife and seven children, and he loved spending time with his family. He was also very generous, and he often gave money to people who needed it.

Sibelius was a great composer, but he was also a good person. He believed in hard work and always tried his best. His music is still loved by people all over the world.

Franz Liszt was a famous composer and pianist who lived from 1811 to 1886. He was born in Hungary, but later lived in Austria and Germany. Liszt was a very talented musician and composed many different kinds of music, including operas, symphonies, and piano pieces.

Liszt started playing the piano when he was quite young, and by the time he was a teenager, he was already a skilled pianist. He also loved to compose music and would spend hours at the piano, creating new pieces. Liszt was known for his ability to play the piano with great emotion and feeling, which made his music very moving and powerful.

Liszt's music was very popular during his lifetime, and it is still loved by people today. Many of his pieces, such as his "Hungarian Rhapsodies" and "Symphony No. 8," are considered some of the greatest works of classical music ever written. Liszt's music is known for its beauty and complexity, and it continues to be performed by orchestras and pianists all over the world.

In addition to his music, Liszt was also a very talented teacher. He taught many young musicians, and many of his students went on to become famous musicians themselves. Liszt was a kind and patient teacher, and he was always willing to help his students improve their skills.

Liszt worked hard and became one of the most beloved and respected musicians of all time.

Taylor Swift is a very popular singer and songwriter. She started making music when she was a teenager and has since become one of the biggest stars in the world. Taylor is known for her catchy tunes and heartfelt lyrics, which often talk about love and relationships.

In addition to writing and singing her own songs, Taylor is also a talented performer. She puts on energetic and entertaining shows for her fans, which often feature fancy costumes and dance routines. Taylor is also known for her kindness and generosity, and she often uses her platform to help others and support important causes.

Over the years, Taylor has released many albums and singles that have become big hits. Some of her most popular songs include "Shake It Off," "Love Story," and "Blank Space." Taylor's music has also won many awards, including several Grammy Awards.

People of all ages enjoy listening to Taylor's music because it makes them happy and helps them to feel good about themselves. Taylor's music is also very relatable, which means that many people can connect with the things she sings about.

In addition to her own success, Taylor has also had a big impact on popular music in the 21st century. She has inspired many other artists and influenced the sound of modern pop music. Taylor's ability to connect with her fans through her music has also made her a role model for many young people.

Henry Purcell was a famous composer who lived a long time ago, in the 1600s and 1700s. He was born in England, and he is known for his beautiful music.

Purcell's music was mostly for the church and the theater but wrote a lot of music for plays and operas, too.

Purcell was also very important as a composer because he helped to bring back the popularity of English music. During his time, most people in England preferred to listen to music from other countries, but Purcell's compositions helped to show people the beauty of English music.

Purcell's music was very different from the music of other composers at the time. It had a special sound that was very lively and energetic. He used a lot of different instruments to create his music. Purcell's music was also very emotional and could make people feel happy or sad.

Purcell was a very important composer because he helped to create a new style of music called "English Baroque." This style was a mix of Italian and French music and was very popular in England.

Purcell also wrote music for the royal court of England. He was the court composer, which meant that he was in charge of writing music for the king and queen.

Purcell's music is still played and enjoyed today, more than 300 years after he wrote it.

Fairuz is a famous singer from Lebanon and is known as the "Soul of Lebanon" because she sings for love, the simple life, for the village and for her country.

She has a huge fan base and her music is enjoyed by people of all ages. Fairuz is also very popular in many parts of the world and has performed in countries like France, the United States, and Canada.

Fairuz has worked with a group called The Rahbani Brothers - Assi AlRahbani, who later became her husband, and Mansour AlRahbani. They have written many of the songs that Fairuz has sung. The Rahbani Brothers have helped Fairuz to become one of the most popular singers in the Middle East.

Fairuz is not only a talented singer, but she is also a kind and generous person. She has used her platform to raise money for various charities and has donated her time to help those in need.

Fairuz has sold more than 150 million records which makes her one the highest selling Middle-eastern musicians of all time and among of the top-selling musical artists in the entire world.

Florence Price was born in Arkansas in 1887. She loved music from a young age and started taking piano lessons when she was just four years old. When she was a teenager, she went to college to study music.

In the 1930s, Florence Price moved to Chicago with her family. She started writing music for orchestras and choirs. She wrote many different kinds of music, including symphonic works, piano music, and songs for choir.

In 1933, Florence Price's Symphony in E minor was played by the Chicago Symphony Orchestra. This was a very big deal because it was the first time a symphonic work by an African-American woman had ever been played by a major orchestra. This made Florence Price quite famous and she became known as a pioneer in the world of classical music.

Florence Price continued to write music for many years and she became one of the most successful African-American composers of her time. She worked very hard to make sure that her music was heard by as many people as possible. She wanted everyone to enjoy her music, no matter what their race or background was.

Florence Price's music is still played today and she is remembered as an important and talented composer. She showed that with hard work and determination, anyone can achieve their dreams.

Gustav Mahler was a famous composer who lived a long time ago. He was born in Austria and grew up to be a musician. Mahler loved music and he spent a lot of time composing and conducting.

Mahler's music was very grand and majestic. He wrote a lot of symphonies, which are long pieces of music for an orchestra to play. His symphonies were so long that they sometimes took over an hour to play!

Mahler was also a conductor and he conducted many famous orchestras all around the world.

One of the things that made Mahler's music so special was that he liked to use a lot of different instruments. He would have the orchestra play all sorts of instruments, like violins, cellos, and even a cowbell!

Another reason Mahler's music is special is because it is very emotional and it tells stories through sound. It can make you feel happy, sad, or even scared. Many people think that Mahler's music is very important because it is so beautiful and it helps us understand and feel different emotions

Mahler was a hard worker and he spent a lot of time practicing and rehearsing. He was very dedicated to his music and he wanted to make it the best it could be.

Sergei Rachmaninoff was a famous composer and pianist from Russia. He was born in 1873 and started playing the piano when he was just four years old!

Rachmaninoff's music is really popular and lots of people still listen to it today.

One of Rachmaninoff's most famous pieces is called the "Piano Concerto No. 2." It's a really beautiful and romantic piece of music, and it's one of his most well-known works. Rachmaninoff also wrote lots of other pieces for the piano, including sonatas, preludes, and etudes.

Rachmaninoff was also a great conductor and he conducted many of his own pieces. He traveled all around the world to perform his music, and he even went on tour in the United States.

In 1917, Rachmaninoff had to leave Russia because of the Russian Revolution. He moved to the United States and lived there for the rest of his life. Rachmaninoff loved living in the United States and he even became an American citizen.

Rachmaninoff was a very talented musician and his music is still loved by people all around the world. He was a master of the piano and his compositions are known for their beautiful melodies and rich harmonies. Rachmaninoff's music is the perfect blend of emotion and technical skill, and it's no wonder why it is still so popular today.

Wynton Marsalis is a very talented musician who was born in New Orleans, Louisiana on October 18, 1961 and grew up in a musical family. His father and brother are also musicians, so Wynton was surrounded by music from a young age.

He started playing the trumpet when he was just six years old and quickly became extremely skilled at it.

Wynton has won lots of awards for his music, including many Grammy Awards. He is the first jazz musician to win a Pulitzer Prize, which is a very special award given to people who make great contributions to the arts.

Wynton has also won a Grammy in classical music, which is another type of music that is different from jazz. This shows that he is an especially versatile musician who can play many different styles of music.

In addition to being a talented musician, Wynton is also a teacher. He has taught at several universities and has even started his own music program called Jazz at Lincoln Center. Jazz at Lincoln Center is a place where people can learn about and listen to jazz music. Wynton has worked hard to make sure that jazz music is recognized and respected as a form of art.

Wynton Marsalis is an amazing musician who has dedicated his life to spreading the joy of jazz music. He is a true artist and has made a big impact on the world of music.

Leontyne Price was a famous opera singer who was born in Mississippi on February 10, 1927. She grew up listening to her parents sing and play the piano, and she started singing and playing the piano herself when she was just a little girl.

Leontyne went to college to study music and then started singing professionally.

Leontyne's voice was beautiful and powerful, and she quickly became one of the most famous opera singers in the world.

She sang in many different languages, including Italian, French, and German, and she sang at some of the most famous opera houses in the world.

Leontyne was the first African American woman to sing at the Metropolitan Opera. She received the Presidential Medal of Freedom, which is the highest honor given to civilians in the United States. She was also made a member of the National Academy of Arts and Sciences, which is a very prestigious organization that recognizes people who have made important contributions to the arts.

Leontyne Price was a truly amazing singer who used her talent to inspire and bring joy to people all over the world. She is remembered as one of the greatest opera singers of all time.

Rita Moreno is a famous actress and singer from Puerto Rico. One of the most impressive things about Rita Moreno is that she has won all four of the biggest awards in the entertainment industry: an Emmy, a Grammy, an Oscar, and a Tony. This is very rare and only a few people have ever done it.

Rita Moreno is a talented actress and singer. She can do many different accents and can sing in different languages. She is also a good dancer and has performed in many stage shows.

Some of the types of music she has sung include Latin music, jazz, and Broadway show tunes.

She is also known for her performances in musical films, such as "West Side Story," where she sang a mix of pop, jazz, and Latin-inspired music. In addition to her work in film and on stage, Rita Moreno has also released several albums of her own, which showcase her talents as a singer and performer.

In addition to her acting and singing career, Rita Moreno is also an author and has written a book about her life. She has had many interesting experiences and has lots of wisdom to share with others.

Rita Moreno has inspired many other actors and singers. She has worked hard to become successful and has never given up, even when things were difficult. She is a role model for people who want to follow their dreams and work hard to achieve them.

ABOUT THE AUTHOR

Larry E. Newman is President and CEO of Children's Music Workshop and the author of more than three hundred music books and musical arrangements written specifically for elementary age students.

His piano, string, woodwind and brass music methods are used in school districts throughout the country. Mr. Newman has taught students from pre-school through university levels and has supervised programs in more than one hundred schools during the course of his career.

Mr. Newman is the recipient of five Los Angeles Area Emmy® Awards for his broadcasts of The All Schools Elementary Honor Orchestra. He wrote, directed and produced the shows which have aired nationally and have featured hundreds of Los Angeles area elementary music students performing in concert from UCLA's renowned Schoenberg Concert Hall.

Mr. Newman was honored by the Los Angeles City Council at City Hall for his contributions to music education in Los Angeles.

As a trumpet player, he has toured the U.S., Canada and Japan with The Glenn Miller Orchestra® and has backed star headline performers in Atlantic City and on the high seas with various hotel casino and cruise ship orchestras.

All of Larry Newman's music books and arrangements are available at **www.musicfunbooks.com**

Printed in Great Britain
by Amazon